DREAM *and* VISION POEMS

DREAM *and* VISION POEMS

Matthew Kraus

Library of Congress Control Number: 2021920533

PAPERBACK: 978-1-956803-15-0
EBOOK: 978-1-956803-16-7

Ordering Information:

For orders and inquiries, please contact:
1-888-404-1388
www.goldtouchpress.com
book.orders@goldtouchpress.com

Printed in the United States of America

Introduction

This poetry may motivate toward and inspire enjoyment of poetry. Be it of a subject, word or word association, these poems are presented for smoothness.

A phrase of a poem connects to the psychology of its subjectiveness. Whether dreams, visions, or something else, a poem's psychological connection may be there.

There are a few types of poetry here. Among the many prose poems are some diagonal poems.

Dreams

Dawn

The dream we dreamt last night was about things of our mystery, we know the night before dawn came as the dream we were into having ended.

We are among those who see the light of dawn as dream time, and after thinking a dawn dream is happening about dawn, surely we see the happiness of dawn dreaming.

Dream

Once someone dreamt up a dream, a dream that reported to the dreamer they were dreaming, the dream worked-on, so dreaming the concept dream was until its time was a dream.

Dream up a dream, please. Otherwise, there is dreaming in the woke-up mental state.

Dreams Plus

Alas! Again there are those dreams where the dreamer needs help. Then, the dreamer calls out, I'm thinking.

The dream answers.

The Dream Vision

The normal visualization of a dream is, one who is into a dream-ramble and perhaps what a normal dream is like, sits. So, let the set of the okay dreams go to what it wants.

It's so one advances to where it is okay, it's so very dreamy.

So freely gone into the dream, its being goes to what it is, dream, which is memorable and looks good. There, it's the assuming dream view gone into the dream.

The wanting to have a lucid dream is really notable.

A room full of dreams is one where we look around. A far room is a place that gets you into the dreamy, cool, grandeur of it. It's surely a dream as strong as that, that brings you peace of mind.

Dream Place

Every night a new dream takes one on, it may seem to ever be heavenly, evening out every such morning's dream place.

The dream took one to where they didn't know where they were. The night before one had the dream, each night, it was a new dream. Each night was a long time of an imaginative dream, of being there and going through each dream center, it is a sip of the drink that says, in every dream that's got a new footing, it's not fooling around.

Wonders

Twenty-seven dream subjects fo to understanding. The belief in facts, going bye-bye, dreaming usual dreams, admiring bird wings, finalizing seeing dreams, a man kindly walking on grass with someone, dreaming of the sea, the feat of self-control, believing in thoughtful dreams, seeing the visions of a dream, things important in a dream, wearing dreamy tights, dreaming of far and wide places, dreaming of being in the wind, going over a bridge, steps going up to a hall, bees, birds, associative dreams, a belief in dreams, your eyes, a new dream wonder, cleaning up, staying dry, time drawing near to a dream going through what has been gone through before as it's going by, mentally being around a dream where the time of what is, and the believable things of dreams.

A final thought, a tight night dream home is nice housing, around it is safety and info on buying dreams. Screening the dream signals tightness in holding onto the dream. In the dream is an expression.

Dream-Theme

Trying to dream, coming to oneness, having a tea, it is a beginning and endures a thought, before the dream dreaming ensues.

Dream Images

At night, purple imaginative events are temptations to dream of everywhere and live a dream life.

Thinking pleasant thoughts of definite, real physical circumstances, corresponding unknown thoughts and words, dreaming is of an identification experience influencing the dream.

Possibilities of certainty type dream are being awake, at play, or imaginatively imaging.

Personalities differ in imagined probable dream realities varying the dream with one's self. The reality of the dream's pleasing indicates experiencing possibilities of good happenings. A dream is better than good, it goes over to even better, and good dreams coming into dream view are remaining beneficial.

Blessed dreams benefit real spiritual experience. For some bit of reality, materializing a dream in the dream reality applauds everything else therein; any form of the definite dream is knowledge of real self-based experience as self-productive protection is in dreaming.

Dream Mind

The dreams that I had were in a mental state of a dream mind. That mind, passing through dream-time there was in the dream mind dream. It's intended to be a fortune. There in a dream, it makes earnest conclusions. Dreams, first and last, are dreamt to dream-life in dreaming. It takes time to convey that way. Special messages dream meanings into meaning a dream, it's like a dream-of-the-day variety.

Sometimes, there is a dream in the mind, the dream there means well.

For The One Dream

Yes, you, the dreamy someone, who has been waiting and looking out for a dream, the dream with someone in it, which is so you are with those there that day, dream.

Then we're there. All so surely, we dream of that someone. We all eventually dream of time as we're sure to look at each other sometime in the dream. We shall go on to dream to see where we are. This is surely the dreaming of one being in the dream, dreaming of the one they dream of.

Dream Show

There was quite a dreamy show put on by the dreamer. In the dreamy show, the dreamer asked if it was a dream. And as they did dream, it was the dreamer's show. One could watch it, so even if it was dreamy for someone, the dreamer, who was in the dream, was okay dreaming. It was dreamy.

Let's Dream

Let's dream. It's a thought dream that lets movement be okay as an upwind bringing on the dreams. They are that okay. Let's dream. It's okay that the dream just goes on and on. In thought-dreams, your thought has it go some way. On it goes. Thought-dreams are all! The dream lets go to the movies you dream. You feel the dreams will take you into the now, which lets you do what you do. It's that dreamy. Soon enough the dream moves on, melting well into its lot. It goes into you and with you. There is no haste, waste, hustle, bustle, hassle or dazzles as we let our dreaming go patterned.

Dream of the House

Naturally, when we dream,
  We go dreamily on, and so we would dream.
    By and by, as we dream,
      Naturally, as we dream as we do. Still
        dreaming? It's
          Our call to the dream world that is
          called the dream of dreams.

Dream Pictures

The pictures of
  The dreams that become
    Sewn into the seams of sleepy tapestries are
      Like a river you've seen in a dream.

Dream of Heaviness

In a dream, one in overnight sleep is hanging heavy clothes on a community clothesline while someone else is taking in their clothes. The one taking in their clothes is hanging out there, also like in a dream, somewhat asleep. Dew had collected on the clothes of the one taking in their clothes from having been there overnight, with that the clothes were heavy. The one in a dream rolled over and returned to sleep.

Dream

Give dreams a chance. Yes! Set that dream free. Let's go to liking miraculous music and guessing dreams are happening. Whatever the dream is, it gets you to dream.

Dream Thought

Dreams should be dreamy thinking so fast. So record it. Misting golden thoughts have so many golden thoughts there it's a weariness in dream. And if the dream's seed expresses the dream while one is wondering, dreaming is what should go on a course of dream. Being too busy to dream is too dreamy a dream to even sometimes think.

Dreams to Morning

Inspired continuance, something we all have, is but a dream. So dreamily ride like a dream riding on a dream. And the dream lay as a way to get the dream. Behind the dream is a lot of the dream. Dreaming was taught by the dreams that melted off to the nearby wings of a folded dream. But where are they all? Where a well psyched-up behaviour of one's path is. A psyched-up, beautiful, dreamy morning dream.

Dream, Unstressed

Dream in the happiness of the dream where someone sees you in a happy dream. The torch of it is, it's a dream.

When someone dreams they are in the norm of loneliness, it has gone better, happiness and dreams are still there.

Does someone, maybe, dream of starlight; shining on in your dream?

Dream-On

Dreaming in a dream-in again, dreamers are trying real hard to dream. So like a dream, a friendly dream's one, some dream is your friend, it's a dream like mine is, where dreaming is in the dream-in is just a dream one has. One has got their hopes and dreams, and then dreamtime starts to slip in and the dream-in seems the dreamer's way. In some ways dreaming is someone singing a song in a dream. Someone is walking along in the dream; they are in the sunshine, the rain and wind. They are in the distance, it's a dream of the dream-in.

Why Dream

Dream purposes are with thoughts, intentions of logic psychologically productive of imagination. Aura-like visualization dreams in dance motion stand out as energetic. A dream moves to dreams as they go into other dreams, gone so that they are okay to be with dreams. If it's that they dream, their visualization is the dear dream itself.

Dream Night

One

Dreams that dream a dream of dreams are some kind of wispy nighttime dream.

Some may yet go on, and so dream.

What the dream remembered was a series of scenes. While the dreaming person slept, the dream dreamer dreamt. The dreamer, who was in the dream, awoke, remembered the dream scene, and went back into a dream.

Awake in the dream, sleeping there was amazing. Then the dreams that were many there opened to the dreamer dreaming into hallways. So every dream there was somewhere there were doors in the hallways. And like a dream of a gentle breath, the prompt of it was that all the dream doorways were swinging open, the dream dreamed this, out of each doorway stepped someone's dream.

Some dreams were wonderful, one dream was dreaming one more dream.

The dream that the dreamy dreamer had was well into the next dream occurring semi-simultaneously. When the one dream connects to another dream and they all start to dream, they are connected to each other.

So when one dream falls forward; they all step out of their dreams. Dreams move through the doorways as though they had been leaning on them.

Dreams that lean against the doorways from which they come are dreaming. And so, yes, a dream falls. The one dream falls to nowhere. That goes nowhere. One dream is a dreamer who fell down. Dreams, they are all there. A dream remained standing, yet, a step further out from the doorway where there was plenty of room, plenty of space. Alive, in the dream, the dream door's dreamers recovered their dreams. And the nice dream of a gentle dreamer prompted dreams in it to be bound to dream. So the connected dreams, bounding, come out and come back to get a dream. Then, dreams dream of time. Revered dreams think that is a thought, a dream was through dreaming and applied itself to medicinal dreaming. The dream that did this was with those dreams connected to other dreams, they were dream-seen by the dreamer.

Two

Deep shadows, they were there. As their dream voices tried to inhabit dreams dreaming of dreams, someone disguised in the dreaminess of a sleep quoted rhymes and smiled. They went on to live forever.

To go those miles, willing slow dreams with thought, dream people went to places and things where all have their dreams. In the idealized beginning was wind, was an end, was a dream meditation idea where singular dreams became plural, where the single dreams that made them plural were the dreams, the dreams went to hundreds. The shadows there did not care while the dream wait went to become a dream home. One wondered whose dream it was. Did time come before the dream? One day was long gone, it went to the long-gone dawn, and the plentiful dreams were dew. And the honey was a dream to dream. It was trying for one to end up dreaming because it was more or less dreaming. Someone was glad they saved their dreams. Dreaming as the dream had its voices was causing someone's harking, there were, while one was setting dreams and dream times free, good that they had dreamt a dream.

Three

Where the dreamer of horoscopic cosmos was at the edge of their ego, that sent the dream off to the dew, the wind caressed the dreamer and someone there, who could have been you.

The dreamer lives in a town, dreams of someone were with the words as their lives lived to dream in words; they could just happen to, by chance. Someone dreams if someone dreams. And then someone dreamed of optical illusions. Someone's dream dreamed of a scene, the dreamer was telling someone that they were of a wild dream; and the dream tone was in such a tone that the dreamer understood the state of the tone. Now, I'm not dreaming one, they said, I'm just visiting with them here. Are you? The dreamer thought, I should not talk like a dream. This is what one might have said, but for food for thought the dream gave them, it would have starved. Today, knowing the value of a dream is dreaming. It's to say that the truth of the dream is a joyous experience. We are at the edge of a stage of dream, the play on the stage is of the dream vibes of the people who are acting in the play. The area is glowing, the dreamer is going deeper into dream. The dream play is about animals, the cockroach, the lizard, and the snake. The dreamer and someone all rely on the food of the dreams. The dreamer would like to keep dreaming as an alternative to blowing responsibilities. Dreaming has its rewards. In their dream, they fly to somewhere dreaming and think, I could have gone into another dream and come back here before. Hundreds, billions of dreams, are everywhere. We sit, we daydream. Dreams set us free. We obviously dream good. And that is such a fine dream. It should be a dream that asks, why dream? The dreamer dreams of a marriage partner and does whatever it takes for them to be as they should be. Someone may ask, why me?

Hundreds of dreams bring the dream closer to dream dawn than the dreamer, or someone is one who could just dream. It's further from dream and closer to love. To dream of thin air is to uncover what is there. Under cover of courage, music dreams of feeling a long life of dreams. I'm trying to have a dreamtime there. There is the dream. It should be drawing near to where its words are that dream sitting in time and staring at the millions of billions of dreams that were in that time gone late into a dream time. If the dreamer were not there nor one in the past, where there was someone, the dreamer inhabiting an abode dream goes to abide where the dream world would, of course, be its life, willing to be a dream. The dream learns of leading, it's carrying on dreaming, the dreamer and someone in the dream. They are dreams, one behind the other, wondering what the ideal dream could be. Then, too, the sky dream and the flying dream go beyond belief, where one could say, this dream may be happening to so many someones and dreamers, that while the earthlings are dreaming of bedtime, their habitations are so healthy, they may go into a dream there, where something is so much anew. The dreams have something to do with very interesting brave things of none-the-less, this is in a dream that nowhere is where to go. It's neither in an either/or dream, nor a star dream, not a windowless sea dream, where emeralds are dreaming to sit in a jar as a dream power. The dream surges, calling the dreamers and someones to dream of wind blowing curtains, wisps of cloud drifting past their ears, which goes into what they hear. The dreamer is outside as almost all of their dreams substantiate, by virtue of the great dream experience, the belief of dream. It's almost overwhelming as part of some dream statement is, it's a pleasurable dream.

Four

Passive dreams are anything in a dream that says, while living becomes dreamy, getting dreamy is a time where we are told that trying to live is a thought. A dream is okay, just so it's a flowery dream of truth and quiet as thought. So then the dreamers, though they dream of the magnificent words of the dream as someone who is content with dreams where they go somewhere, it's a thought of the dreams. New dreams know the dreamer is wanting to dream. Being around a time of dream and dreamy things is all but what would be this dream. It would seem an abstract dream is so obtuse that the necessities of dreams following in flowing patterns are dreamt as, companionable to the life of a dream, the following dreams, which are the ones that are what one would expect in a dream, where the dream is seen.

Start Emptiness

In fine times of a dream lay somewhat as rhymes starting a division of the emptiness, such that each time it's by an emptiness of the dream in the replacement of some of them, the emptiness of the one dream is with an abundance of absences that start the emptiness and go into a point of no return.

Back

Well, having almost found out why one comes to dream is, it's a dream of being back there to dream. Have you ever experienced the dream where doubt doesn't exist, where light is so when you know it's when you dream, that's your place? It's the right place to dream, that is where it's at. Coming from going too into a dream, all the time dreaming has been a way to believe being enlightened by it is involved in some sort of dream is the dream. The dream is a course to its only being where you may dream to have the dream.

There, it's a long, long sign. Where the dotted line is for your dream, you are the dream. That dream enjoys that you came to it, dreaming it was the way. And rhyme had it; you'd go back to where it, in fact, was a dream.

Dream On

If you look at what you've dreamt when your dreaming has gone, remember somewhere some of the joy of dreaming may be joyfully waltzing you through the dream sky; and the dreamer thinks, the dreams go through the sky's avoidance of you're-the-only-mystery.

The dreaminess is when someone is foolish. And that dream goes to know feelings; however the dream feels, it's the dreams that come then, they come into a time to be a dream. When someone dreams, they know it makes sense to dream, they look at their dream and think.

In time, a dream makes a long haul of taking one to a just so long to dream dream. It would be like finding the dream is an answer to the question while we get the meaning of a dream. It's perhaps what is going on, in a dream. It's so vision-like.

Doing what the dream is doing, going on to where the dream goes, asking a question, dream again, up in the dream sky it's like a feeling of an occasional dreamy, cool breeze. It blows through the now blue dream sky way. You may see it's there and like a dream, it's a refreshing dream. The dream breeze goes as it goes to a blue sky dream like a jet stream, like it's another dream breeze blowing. And one should be dreaming.

Only thought is dream to dream, and for you, dream to like the dream breeze; wonder how many times awake in the night before waking to find you are speaking those words of dream come true.

And alive for the day, awake to try and tell you it's the same for you as then, when the dream and sleep are cool.

It's true to wake-up. Sometimes again in the time of feeling alive there is a well awake feeling. It's a good, cool wind. Feel the dream breeze and feel it as it blows, making no mistakes, through the trees.

And at ease, where there is a dream, there is wonder.

You want to climb trees from seeing them and their green leaves. A dream wants to feel whatever and waits to please and pauses to sleep.

Lucid thought goes from that which was in the dreamer's soul. In wanting to dream, wanting to go more-so dreaming; may you know you too, who tried dreaming, dream! Keep thinking of the you nobody knows. For like you who do dream, it's to a dream.

We, who don't know which way the dreams go, blow our sleep, which is why the rocks roll if they go dreaming. And when a rock rolls, rocks may dream it's rolling free when sleeping. Like rocks loose on a rocky hillside, our dreams know, since that makes us sleep.

We also dream as a wave finally breaks. As the dream wave breaks and rolls on to shore it is what is, that it was a dream was a dream!

It's that dreamy of a night, make no mistake, it's there for free. You can dream. Dream classy if that's for you. Can you know which dream has anything? Dream until the wake time sun, credited for every dream that one has.

Thinking quick, water is fun when you dream. It's well there, stared at when tried. A dream, it is so much.

It seems well, thought the dreamer. It seems we dreamt everything one could; dreamt as standing on wood, on branches.

The cold dream was tired when water was coming down in it and we were too over it when the wind was on the ground, it's blowing through the trees. And the time crept through forests of slime-covered rocks, dead trees in places rather forest-deep, getting where down is up is where it's been. Then, where the lost seem lost, dreams see the enlarged view, then hurried and typed, dreaming, having gone through it all, even with the love we've been true to, it has all been a dream of lost loves gone too far in the dream.

See the brown, black, and blue, see the red, white and blue, too; from the heights of thought. There never was a bad word for you, seen, until it wasn't time to for a forest of hues be there. Heard the enlarged scenes are vision-hued mirrored mysteries. On, that's the moon of it. Like when the tides are held-up, to be gone is true, it's so far a dream from where we had a thought of them. That was when they were there, when it always went to always. And one dream thing went to be from all it was, such things as those to hold on to are to dream. Like the mysterious mission for the mystery missions, dreams lost to be on, where on carpeted forest floors there are thoughts of the wind tossed leaves, they were dreams lost like a fine dream that was there. They were dreams like fine times in the leaves of the tops of trees. And as dreamers lost dream sight they lost sight of their thoughts.

Birds loved it there, it was like the visual scent of a rose.

In a muck, like the luck that ran through it, then-dreaming was so beautiful. In that, it was all there, cool. Far away from that state of dreaming, which could dream it cried flight; it was to see the heavens above. For the sky, it was loving the dream.

Evenings to mornings, doses of dream came and dealt their dreamers a boon.

Dreaming was soon a gain, which was so high a mountain that a sweet air dream was there. So we had to fly on, it was like a bird's flight. With wings, you're so high that to turn around and run, which is an effortless thing to do, is a natural dream. And in all of that, it was cool. It was so far away from that state of dream that could not be, that flying in it all, it was okay to dream.

But the assumed dream flight is to the heavens above to see the sky, which turns to the pure love of an evening's tomorrow. That comes into the places like those dreams that are so it can rain.

Quiet trumpeters herald the sky's opening, a dream.

And maybe a daily dream would be sleep that may alter the beddings on which dreamers are tossed. If a hammock is there, then it is of that fresh country dream, its airs so into the lantern lit hills of a dreamy nearby sea below of which it may have been possible to hear a bird's call. Dream of it yet, or two.

Then, maybe it will stop and step itself out of a hall, or hail to a hall, someone in there is full, and someone is on a trail. So far, for someone to come quietly by the countryside, someone observes one is in all that one sees. You see that in all of the freshness of the freedom of the sea. You see there, the companion.

The dreamer with lucid dreams slows to say, as if it was someone who was well remembered, who knew what it was, things. It's a place where that might be what it is of, it's a dream. We might uncover lovers in poems, music, dreams, and song, but as the looked at theories of art are bringing the dreams, the dreamer is going through time-dream and sleep-think.

It is what it is, and that is with the trumpeting.

You ask, are your dreams had, bad or good, which are of the dream that is to be added to, or is it upon the case of the dream havers and those places that have the gift of dream and wake to ask something?

How would one consider the work dream's pleasures? While there is no denying thoughts, they are there. Then, they might be like another dream type of slogans like dream if you do and dream if you don't; dream well if you do dream, and dream well if it's your want; if you want. But dream if you do, it is dreaming that is capable of enlightening one.

The dreaming is undoubtedly where there is a thought.

After that dream someone could express dream feedback, dreaminess and sense.

Thought dreams on another dream planet, or hopefully better put dreams, it is but someone's mind that is turning to dream. Oh, so it goes well if hands are holding dreams. Were it icy then, one would wonder if there was a so lucid dream. And who might it be enlightening? It could be upon squeezing the wakefulness of lucidity, dreaming rain.

Would it be heard of there, would it be there if it were the truth that actually existence was a dream? Yet dreams do feel it. It is so prevailing, it must be a dream. Then, it would be wanted, would be best delivering lucidity to a dream as one is dreaming.

Yes, yes to a dream's will; yes, it's such a dream will. It is willing to be what it is, too.

Then that might be a kick in some dream. How would one consider it if the dream was so simple that it dreamt, yet it would know. Dream, but wouldn't it be understanding and dream to be well? Then, should a dream have to go broke? A dream is or isn't this piece of that incomprehensible, incomparable puzzle?

Then, you might be able to fill it in with water and wood, cement and glue, paper and paint, or plaster and paint. It sounds like a recipe. Or dream if you've a thought, it's like a drop in a well. You ask, well, if it's in between the starlight and glitter, or the blue sky and the twinkle of the light of the stars as they dream, seeing the sights that are there, then, the dreamer wonders in their dream soul, sometimes, that is what it is: as lucid as deep, it's so sometimes that dream is more-so other than the time that might be there, little what it dream might be if these dreams were poems heard, or a hundred thousand or so, so the dream poetry may be one of the many? It's so odd, before when there was the dream that was a passageway in sleep; there was a dream poet's name to them. There, in the dream, when there is that dream, which is like a beginning dream; the dream is there, is then. It might be of a heavy time, a dream of those with their dreams in their back dreams, dreams thrown to be gone like with a dream sling, it's like those thoughts, like things that are there are dream. It is gratuitous that dreams, taken as they surely could be, and a dream of a handshake in its thought that it's like a bee's dream. And as it could be from a dream, a file, or a map, living a dream like a fly, like the ostrich, the dream through its smiles to the dream of a camel with its mileage, is all there is. As it's as dreamy as there is, that is with the verbal tenses, the language all goes like it's a laugh and dream was to beware of an ink pen. That is too short, so it, the dream, sees the paper on a table, and the dreamer's thoughts of another kind of dream administration agree, all is well. So dream into a kind of dream school so that all is blue, as it can be a dream it's as well as a hand held paper, the dream from which one sees there is meaningful times.

Times are in these things, in these dreams, three then, there are things that they would seem to come to dreaming quickly, they're from the past, they go to where the dreams are. Of those that file past is one dreaming in their dreams, while it's all of its inflight dream to meanwhile have a dream, it has a dream. Dreams sitting there say, what else is there for us to do but dream-go from one dream to another dream, sweet though they may be. They say to the dream, who are you there? They answer, we are driving the dream someone has, and to go down to the well-up-the-hall dream, it's there when it's all down the hall where everything is a dream, there is a waiting until the dream is a mist.

The dreams that are sweet remain in memory like flour on a kneading cloth after the loaf has been given to bake. A dream, it twists! Tinkling so lightly, the dream of floating is there, you capture it and fly like a bird, it is energizing you as a dream of sleep, passing.

The time you had some dreams was that. That is what is intense. It's sitting easily on a dream, it's flying onto the dawn as it can be a dream. As it flies, the dream becomes lazy as the sleeping dreamer, sleeping less intensely, is with the people that dream. They would be in a dream there if they mentally were able to. They search the dream for the answer to the dream. In that the dreamers could find the meanings, dream-thought is wonderful!

As that dreamer can be the dream answer to the dreamer's quest, the night dreams await!

When the dream-answers are in the same place as their truth, it's the revealing of itself, it's as love, it's with the anonymity of a previous dream, and it's as the past, which is like the promise of a dream. The broken dream finds it is like a whole dream, yet it's like the leaves on a tree that fall in season, there are as many dreams as there are wanted. Dreams, with the dreams filing past, dream companies of dreams, doctor's dream too; they are there but good at getting groovy! Then, right when they are about to dream, they climb a dream ladder and dream of the moon where there are yet honored and spaced dreams. They have it, dreams are too soon becoming dream savvy. Then, to dream is to do with some of the problems of being the dream there, which is a dream becoming known. One finds it would be a golden key, that dreamer's interpreter, who opens a hope to the dream. The door is the answer to all the unanswered questions that may be there. Would the dream there be only that dream, or could one, because of the dreams, dream?

In the clear times of dream are those that strive, they who are just too few dream though it is a dream that is clear. With the eye of truth, the dream interpreter knows that it's so, a dream in that is just like a piece of paper that says, to be a dreamer, someone, it is well to keep your own thoughts, and that is a dream.

That dream may be there, as in the way of the dream of the blue-high sky so that dream-way is when there is a dreamer, there. You are the you where you hear that dream, although you know the cause of a dream is of a cause you only know.

The cause of the dream is if it sounds like a dream, it's a game.

As it's only like someone's elementary dream, it's a dream of water, it's that which one sees. You see it's you who are there, the dream wills it to be there; then you fly. Yet, if the element of the dream flies, as it will, it may go, maybe to see, you see the value in it.

It isn't sarcasm, especially since it your fame that explains in a dream.

It may be why someone is all that they are.

So the dream-time gone a way to being time that's there, a time for a course of dreamers as laziness is so right for feeling the not lazy lay, but away from a falling dream as it should be. One dream is onto you, but you like the time.

As it has a moment, a dream that has positiveness is there.

It should be a rising dream and a falling dream so they'll say that the dreamer is rising as one would. It's not rising like the Big Dipper, it's a dream about to sign off. But, like the sky, which is in the present time, it's able to stand it. It's about to go on longer than dream-thought, the Big Dipper knows how to dream that is what it is, it is going to a vanishing art.

The mind of the dream had the nerve to go, more-so, to what it is. What that dreamer had gotten, it has gotten by light, there, more-so there, which is hoped for. A prayer of dreams, dreams like to pray for that dreamer, who is one with the dream. They will be with us today.

Could they dream and pray for some dream to come true, better?

You say it is so good. Some may say that is cool, some may say it is kept groovy. The dream mood for you is when your dream is free, it's to say what it is. That it has been a mindful dream, like a dreamer's hope is like living to dream is living to sing. And keeping the dream in mind, you sit on it like it's a way of day-dreaming, wondering if it's a dream that is vitality or if that is your dream as you dream away.

Sleep Dream

Long dreams and sleep-dreams continue with the lost, last trumpet sounds. And the freedom of thought lets the eternal ring of thought throughout there, where happiness is in years of cloister-ages comes too close for the time being that brings dream.

A sleepy dream whisper, hazy dream, long and dream continuing with lost thoughts, lasts, which is like a trumpet's sound ringing out.

A Dream Night

Someone, their dream in their thoughts, is one who ever laughs in their dreams.

They sleep peacefully. And if someone is well bedded, in bed and they're so alone at night sleeping, they're one, alone, they are whoever has a thought about what they dream. They live to dream one dream, which lives to the end.

Someone is Dreaming

Something seems to always get one dreaming, so when one is dreaming one wakes up and finds someone is there! Its wild when one is sleeping and they know it's a dream.

There is a dawn. The time goes by!

When one knows they're dreaming, it's a nightly dream, one knows that somebody cares about them. And then it's a dream sleep one has caught up on. If one is sleeping and there's a long gone dream, when it's a dream because one has caught up on one's sleeping, someone is dreaming.

When one is dreaming, it's sleeping.

Someone is dreaming! It's one dream that always gets one to sleeping, which is a dream when they're sleeping, it's a dream for someone who likes dreaming dreams.

Dream Way

I want my body to dream because it's a dream way, way out. Come to dream and see that's where you like to dream it, it is such a dream way-far out, where you dream way-out. There are kids who are all gutsy, way out. While the dream is always looking for grooving, it's in the hot, lazy way-out self.

Dreams have made their way. The dream is to go on, way out.

Dreams all have ways, the dream is solid! Dreams are good.

Someone says dream this while getting it on. Doing what they're dreaming of, it's as if ever when you stoop to pick up something, it'll be in that rain's footsteps of dream as rain pounding on the roof! Way out!

Room Dream

An actuality that this dream thing does belong to someone is the one thing one dreams. And when one sleeps there and rests their natural dream thought, it is a sincere dream. In opinion and experience, the average, lucky work is dreaming. Luck is monetarily lucky. The dreams are like water, they are in a dream room. Think. Most thoughts have some poverty in them! A dream is better put in writing. A personal, mean, little dream likes it there in a room. Point is, matters of consequence to the dreamer presume the dreamer is dreaming.

In another dream, this thought, remembrance is thought, though it was a dream and the dream that dreamed it was a room the dream belonged to.

A person, actually dreaming, is resting.

Then, to go on to a natural life of eating, living and dreaming, experiencing the opinion of a dream is all. After luck, money dreams. Just saying it has gotten personal so that there is no consequence in a dream, to dream meets up in a dream with the adventure, which to the insight of fond time that looks out, dreams. The dreamer was dreaming where dream rooms supported the dreaming. For that, anyone who would be dreamy after all saying dream is just basically existent and in the flow of dream is in a room that has been and is having a dream.

Wellness Dream

It's a wellness dream note, a familiar new dream, dream are dreams.

Well, perhaps a mate, a stranger in the scene, seems like a strange dream, apparently so good.

That dream is a boon.

Here letters escape thoughts, inner dreams, gilded as in a next thought relieve being ultra-shallow. Though it is such a sleep, it is not that lost. You must allow yourself time to breathe and dream. There, meditation on dreaming is sleeping. Napping is the thing. It is a dream to have believers there. It's so talented. For one to believe in their dream in a nighttime dreaminess that goes far beyond dream wellness, where cool as a breeze is a dream as well, it goes well.

Well, dreams are seen now as wellness like a wellness in excess of dreamtime where time is the only well being thing. An ability to be well is a wellbeing dream. In a time so wonderful, people in dreams, who breathe and see the stars, are good dreaming until late, dream laziness.

Wellness dreams. A wellbeing dream is well, perhaps meditating that strangeness for a dream mate is nothing but deep sleeping and dozing. Napping as guiltlessness is a dream. There in the next dream of a time, it goes on to another wellness dream for a while.

Well, dream. Dream some other dreams. Hear wellness dreams. Some people in dreams, they go to wellbeing throttle, it holds at dream one when time only seems a strange thing to escape to. To see the dream dream and the dreaming has its wellness, one sleeps well.

Dream well. Dream it where dream's inner thoughts are a holiday. And belief is that which lends its wellness dream to the test. What must be a dream time is and will ever reveal when dreams escape time. Lost in the dream wellness, time goes past the present.

It feels like being beyond the dream is a dream. The dream you hear of is the dream you see.

In time, the wellness of a wellness dream goes on. Is that somewhat a strange dream?

To dream of a holiday with fresh air, sleep and birds singing, find time to dream. Dreaming is an escaping dream; it's a wellness dream where time goes and dreams.

Painter Dream

Pastel painting says:
  A dream,
    Wonderful comes onto canvas. I am
      Dreaming a dream, a dream that has gotten
        to my side of thought.

The Dream

The dream, it's cool. Cool to sleep, it's a dream, compelled by a power greater than the dreamer. The dream moves what it wants to, to steal away in a dream.

Sea Star Dream

When the sea sees through its open doors, stars, the sea-dreams of stars, it's the place to dream of sleep, for you do what you can do, and it isn't too late to dream.

Never Until Dream

When one came to the camera of the mind that dreamt of getting through to it all, even though the film of thought was looking real good, it was dreaming. That was when it was asleep, right until it was that dream night, when like a dream that felt so right, it felt a flight. While the cold-felt dream was real good, it was all really red hot and blue, so the dream dreams through it all and the cool of the flight was with the night. The dream felt like the treasure of the dreamer too. As the dreamer felt the feet of the dream it was all jest. And so the best it could do, without making a song, was to come along. In the dream, there was a bird building its nest upstairs in a dream.

Your Dream

You should know that the dream of now is the now in which wherever you know a dream has a way to go, in the blanket of dreams that holds onto the time the dreamer knows how it is now. It does go to dream.

Fourteen Dreams

Fourteen dreams start out dearly, cold in the heat of a hot summer. With a cool dream thought, the dreams that were alive were flowers at the start of the dream and the dreams immersed one in a well fathomed well of flying where it's full dream is sleepy. The dreams might try all-one-night to find the reward of hope in a fine dream, and in that sleep there, as a dream produced by bees, they become aware that the next dream is there.

Open the Book

If you can open the book without a look, it may be perhaps tomorrow you'll wake in some of your dreams. If you wait till late for your fate, as someone who is late, a dream of someone waiting for you fits into the picture. One dream thought is picking up on it here, there's enough dream-time for all to be in it there. And while dreaming to be there without someone maybe like thinking it's a dream, the book dream is so like time. So like the centuries of time that are turning on, pages of the history book, dreams close in on the time that depends on its being there. Whether it's dream or dreamy, the point is: open the closed book to where the dream is waking from dreamy sleep.

Dreamer Dreams

The awake dream tried eyeing the adults who found they lost a smile in trying to be smaller. The wide eyes were awake, and the vision dream nearby was rewarded most often as were most of those who dreamt. And ever were they rejuvenated for dreaming.

Dream Arts

Once, dreams were related to nothing. And it seems they have their connections to living. So, there is a path on which they go. We go dreaming our dreams, once.

They are in our dreams. One finds time when trying to find a different way to be there was a question. If it was something to know, you might be who once was there. But it kept the dream from the going on inside toy, where a dream is a balloon filled with water. Who knows, in loving brightly, if the peace of cool feeling is a dream. Once, when there was something new there, one wanted to receive it to resolve it if something one might find would be: once upon a time.

The Dreamy Place

There once was a dream, a dream place. People lived there, it was a lot like a dream town where dream people were dreaming. It is time that gropes the grapes, rained on. By that, for one dream or the other, the dream was one. And though the dream is fruity and bleak, the dream is on top where there is no one more dreamily written of than the dream of now. As the dream is inside the dream, the dream gets confused. The dream gushes in the make of some dream, where dream is its only companion, and smiles hear that dreams disperse like rot going to dust.

Tree Dream

One dream on the way to see its tree is a dream on the way to dream. If one dream is on the way and the dream finds one dream is on the way, it's okay.

Over Dream

Sleep one morning and you dream of sleeping too late. The dream has a fatalistic dream that dreams it ought to be dreaming. And so going deeper into sleep reminds one of mornings, dreaming goes too late and sees the dream. Whatever the dream philosophy may be, whenever the dream wants to dream see, dream.

Tune Dream

The start of the dream, counting, is of the past. And like the dream that lasts, the dream is more like music than a rustic remiss. If the dream starts music, it allows the dreamer to continue to the end of the tune and dreams.

Sleeping While Dreaming Tonight

Dreaming, so sleepy and tired dreaming began as sleeping, while the tonight dream psych up dream is within our home, able to sleep and therefore dream. So closely dreaming to come through to this thought of it, so dreaming it seems so present, while dream-thoughts fly and pass by, on no dream, yes, that's the dream way. It is soon, we find a chance to dream, run, and exercise. And tomorrow, perhaps, dream.

You will see me, too, dreaming as you are dreaming. All the way to where the dream is. It's the way you are. But do dream as much as that. And one is able to.

Even to go on in a dream, one goes to work.

Dreaming is carrying thoughts on. And like a friend being around, soaking up the peace and whatever determination to dream may be there, the dream we like is back where it was. It was hard there, yet dreaming to go somewhere so far away is with the relief of dreaming of nowhere. Wherever the road leads is the possibility of walking on it to its end. Notices of that dream end is where the drip dream drains, which has been where men doing that are but the night that allows dream. Sleep away, as there is much to say again, when dreaming is a dream and sleeping is business as always.

Eternal Dreams

What would you see in dreaming of an eternity?
    Would it be a tube television in black and white,
        a train track alongside a wide river,
            a rack fastened with a tack for a hat,
        Or a sack of starry stares shimmering,
      Taking care of the dream, which has a psyched
        up view
    Of a visionary dream mystique, a dream where its
    hues

And the truth of the dream believes the dream is singing, reliving dreams.

A Dream

Dream of the dream world. Of the dream. That's what the haven dream meant one day as it came along singing a song, dream a dreamy one.

Recurring Dream

Again and again and again, a dream that came to be seen as the dreams were dreamy and grave dreaming was the same, symbols of dreams were thoughts of the one dream, we. Like the dream rest, while catalogs and cats call, dreaming is doing the dream. Just plan on that dance, and dream through those dreams. That's the never seen dream some say, the ever seen dream way. That's it. It was a dream, just doing its thing, and done dreaming too, those dreams that were quite caught up on the time the dream took, take a look and dream.

And Dream

The wind dream whispered ut-oh, the world dream dreamed of it too. That was once a mentality. It went roaring into a-calamity. But the same name, highly likely that dream goes to the spot, caught a lot of the dream that roared. I'm whispering wind dreams and I've got to be getting about. While the roaring dream shows its back and both of the dreams want to holler, the dream roars, it's blowing its dream life into dream some more. Where a whispering dream roars of the dream shattering the dream and the dream, which is gone whispering, is like the wind dream, dream whispering. Wherever the dream glory has gone, its time has left with it. The pieces of the dream, left to be dreamt again, which are blown by the leftover dream to the right of where it was is the dream it tried to be as a spin-off of the dream on a yet getting the mind of the dream to out-of-sight without blowing the dreamers mind and in fact bringing them to blissfully pause in happy relief.

On Through A Dream

A dream starts deadened cold, surprised that its start is old, starring a dream cat that blows away in a hat ahead of the dream. All of which is with a real start. That is, it happened as a dream.

Life Dream

The dream of a love of life, living the dream, psychically present, and around a dream's dream is where it was, trying to dream some. Then, as the living dream, told a loving life, go slow to be the love of life, and as the freeload of life, dreaming, it was all that is. It was freely dreaming to be a bold life load and the thing of it was very heavy. Dreaming of flying free with a load of life, understanding there is a dream able to see, wary that the load of feeling free is a dream.

Dreams to the End

Dreaming to the end of consciousness, the subconscious, friend, is the child of the unconscious with meanings. Hidden in it, is the fate of the dream, that is to wake and find the mind that is a friend, to dream to the end and have consciousness. Subconscious unconscious people dreaming through meaning is some kind of a merry time dream. Fair to the end, the collective unconsciousness of dreamers have a focus of the mind end. It's what we wear as we dream a dream.

Dream Fare

Dreaming that has such a far distance to go meets an even more different being there. It's life like; it goes on at all costs. Beginnings there have a trip to go on, with memories. So memory dreams are lots of picking up healthy ways to ride, when all good is fair, and the dream is people are fans for it. Really.

Radio Dream

The dues, while there are dreams around and if one thinks it's a goodness going on, are that there is a dream around a dream. While the people paying dreams of their own may see some may put their dream in the dream found. While the news is mentioned, its but in the lot that stays where it is, a found dream on the ecool dream radio stays dreamy and the radio dream that pays for the dreams had the blues. If the radio dream says some news is good, while the Hollywood dream may say it's the show, and the show pays for it then, there are a lot of dreams where people stand in line to pay their.

Dream Dawn

We, who believe a mysterious, nightly dream gives us a dawn, are in one another's ego. We say, we know our group ego, on the way to the dawn through a dream. Time shows us the last dream was the night before. And that dream is you, dreaming, you, who see the lights of day, dream.

After the dawning of a dream one is thinking! Thinking of dawn, we dream of sleeping through dawn. So we dream to go to such a dream time. A dream that is so well, and if we are being worthy of the dream,

45

Dreams

There is a grace of dream relief, a relief from normal tension that is so a dream like lucid dream trance! The accompaniment of time of that dream is seeming as could be, a usual, typical scene.

The scene that is accompanying you is of your dream time.

It's good if there's no recurring dream.

Visions

Flowing Streams

Streams! Amid the effortlessly flowing streams, breathe dancing, by chance you drive through the happy sound of their trickling. The brooks of life flow and the stream flows into its own, taking you into its arms. As an artist's canvas is mysterious untouched, as a ship has a sail powerfully unfurled, stream headwater takes a while to become the present magic moment of stream flow. The love of headwaters is born and the birth of them is their flowing, telling of the love of streams for stream headwater, a change of dance chance.

Three Flowers for Ships

Three flowers scale up to ship size, their petals are at least different from the vessel. The flowers for ships are for shipping actually sweet as honey, and the bees would be, despite hundreds of ways of looking at it, each time at least a little different. The flowers cover a stony brook side showing you the way the stream looks at it, the ship is but a small canoe and there are flowers for the canoe to go wherever guiltlessness rolls on.

Breath

Breathing enlightens. One was quite well breathing as the door before it slammed, which was well before it was running out, on and on, which kept the one quite like the old door. The door, sure sensing it was made to be, it was as it was, going to clues. There is where it was sure it knew the ins and out of it. The ins and out of it really went to get the in check of its points clear, which got to be touched.

In with the breath of it, which was the body breathing, the door was a favorite part of breathing. All you have to do is have a mean breath rate, a numerical analysis of breathing gone to its meaning, the door, which is a little more like what you've got when it is what that is, and the view to do it. So, if anyone has got it, and it's worth thinking of, the lot will get the taste of door deep breathing. You've got the touching end of it down so well! So give it to the top of the limit of the mean breath. Breathe. And so, if you are liking it and it's something to be aware of, it's a classic then.

Feeling like the view that is in the door, it's a view that allows us through, by breathing, to go in and out to where, now we are into the air view. It's so you and me that we keep holding on to the touch of it while being there with us being there. It's your view, it's my view, it's a view in you, it's a view into me, its breath, and it's breathing.

Mysterious Ocean

The mysterious ocean was that way because it was the end. The mysterious ocean was one that had a friend. The mysterious ocean was mysterious, the way it tossed and turned.

Is it like a mermaid, mysterious while other possibilities are just fine?

There are many mysteries of this that are conscious like. Then there are many more mysteries and oceans that are there at times and aren't either way.

If you get my drift, another mermaid answered.

But since the mystery of an ocean is the ocean and a mystery, there are those that wait there as many are of this sort of thing too; as the two chirp mysteriously, the ocean does shake.

And an ocean is the end. The meaning of the ocean is a mystery that may be clear, though some others are less like a mystery and then. And while the oceans are not always very clear, days go by like meanings that have some sort of bearing. While some meanings wake where some meanings are like the world's own quake, earthquakes that wake one send some oceans swirling into the light. The cool thought is, some oceans are shaking. Indeed, as they do, the mere thought is a clue! Though some oceans then are bright and the mysteries are clear, the behavior of another may be like the other, to an ocean dear.

It is enough to cause the mystery.

And so shaking it became clear there is an ocean and a mystery having fun. There are many mysteries for someone who has time, in a morning's ocean mystery is the sun. The sun's a way to a time that seems like an ocean, and the ocean lasts a long while. A long time for an ocean to sit. While, of course, its end is mysterious, isn't?

The Wish Vision

The vision wish fulfillment: Coconut palm leaves grass rustling sound as rainbows and rainfall dripping, rainbows, rainbows connecting land to sea through mirrored reflection. The land of hills and streams, a soft wind blowing over dew, soft rain raindrops background, a footbridge across a stream, slender ponds beside a stream, wishing wells. Long the vision you may have.

Suggestion, a Vision

Take a suggestion, do what you want. Listen, if you're in a spot, take a suggestion to do and to be what life is suggesting to you and to me. Life is someone speaking, it's perhaps environmentally suggesting, listen for ideas. Listen, you're in a spot. Like pushing a button or stubbing a toe, maybe you've a big job so no one, no one among us, will know. Listen well, you're in a spot, take a suggestion, do what you want. Slowly suggesting, it makes no difference, you know the show of suggestion will be fine. Though it could be slow or fast it could be a dream, it could be a crash test. Anyway it's a scene. Take a suggestion, it's a probability, or is it a suggestion, a possibilities scheme.

Do what you want to? If you are in a spot and like taking a suggestion, take a suggestion to do what you want. Take a suggestion, the suggestion, which is so free, it may go being thought of as a bunch of words like leaves drifting in a bright breeze.

Scarecrow Mind

The scarecrow, like a man, like an echo, suggests the scarecrow is a person and so scary. The dummy scarecrow portrays man.

A farmer says, you should know, to this crop.

To the birds, the scarecrow says, you should know to go away from the green-colored leaves of corn.

In the instant they are told, this frees their ambition, they have to believe this, the scarecrow frees their ambition. They win the mind so fine and find a trying mind.

The scarecrow mind asks itself, what am I doing?

The view of it tells all, before leaving. The mind asks to go where it would be going if where you go is where one would go?

And one doesn't know where they are going. But they all uniquely see the vibrating sky is alive and are flying.

What Is

What are the sphinx, the eye, a million microscopic scenes, a looking glass, a watery nest, a headrest, or a placid field, a colored lantern, a closed door, a wall in a room, a road, a flower house, flower in bloom? Things.

What is it to think, is it within the sight that is seen? These are in, they go to a within the mind. And it's possible that without these things in between, like a sweet, sweet event, it is what it may have to be, nonchalant thought.

Meanwhile Start

A sizzling fire, a match shot rang out is like a footrace's false start. To light a laugh, like a participant waiting to race on the audience pensive, Meanwhile, the match being at a free zinging place in time sits static as the two racers about to go go off.

Voice Visual

The voice visualized saying it is saying that it's heavy shaking, it feels free and it's, baby, oh, so cool. Like a woman and her baby, it's that nice. It's what it is, it says, it's all so right. And, so what is it you're doing? Is that what the truth is? Have you asked to be in the lonely crowd? That's it if its feeling is likely true, and you keep hearing a voice going, baby, go on through time.

One tends toward a visionary of the youth, the what the crowd suggests.

Reeling Wave

The mind that is reeling from the view of an ocean's wave hears it is like a whistle, once you hear that, it is there. Thousands of bells, shells turning on a beach tinkle with the receding of a wave. Like the sound that dwells in a shell, the reeling wave is a world away. The world of waves is, you surmise, it doesn't, have that much to say to you. You smile away, wink of a wave, reeling, as the sound is made.

Movement Moment

Movements towards the happy, hopeful moments, magic portrayed, move anything toward a realized past, where what existed in pictures is ever the pictures that are never there.

On

A dream to start a view dissolved when it is all that, which was a vision that went well into just being plain fancy and new.

A fancy view, it's all-dissolved into a vision.

Nest Egg Vision

As the role model of having a nest egg is good, an illusion above some thought, the illusion wings and increases something of the nest egg substance. It's, nevertheless, to get a flight of thought favor, and being a real vision it seems so free, that it's with a fee-like squeeze.

Game Up

Well one, a well full, yet missed, is in a spot. Cleaning one's my ring, a hot shot up in looking about it's calling to the visionary in one, planing into the future. Ever to see-dream again, ever to be free with the words that you please, you couldn't find a better time than now to progress in mind to the following, it's showing you there is a way, so rather than go away from the flurry, we'll probably be the better by playing some mind game, and wish. Rather than calamities, it'd be better than a wish.

Dead Start, Lost

A closet opened and out of the dark into the light, a heavily clothed choir of twenty-one or so angels; pure, clean, blessed sang. They sang brightly, lightly, songs in song forms from the song starts, A song to the tomes of the sky, of the hall of lost songs is in those closest to the sky, penetrating light song.

Still Green

Seconds were lost in the feverish pitch of what one saw, hailing a green pasture bounded by silly, green mirrors; still the mirror surface of some ponds forming dreams from somewhere.

At Once There

At once, there were services of the inn that included air. They said, there have been some customers that look too like you. Some are you. But since we believed in your paying your bill on time, it won't get to us. So, as it's over and goodbye is a rose, clover is growing and everything is covered. So you can't get something started until your courage is behind it, when that is all gone, do you think it's over? A thought is they ought to just fly around, but on the questions of it's so their's a blessing while you're thinking of something else. You walk over the ground like a frosty snowman and find a big fish, which you want to have in a drink, then you're by the sea. A year before there were white-coated mailmen, in some places that were airy they were taking notes while you tried to get there. Where men were covered with sauce like dressings and you were alright since the salad was quite tossed, you rested.

With food came the season when trees wore red linen, and stamps were where somebody waits in a line, the deep freeze cough is there.

It's a look out where a person who is into a fifty-ninth cab trip, it's much of the day and a manager is on the side waiting to be in the frost. A dip in it is, it's caught up on time, while climbing some trees there, are other thoughts that are of the lot of the day. Dew on the trees is talking to you who became lost into getting polka dot dress, and that was a grate in the way that it was. Then the law said it was plain there were fruit on the trees, and saying to all, it's worse than that, they're saying it's a scene. But it can't be seen since it is seeming to be alluding to the other special things. So sitting there knitting with knitting needles with curved hooks, you think there's a chance you're mode of existence caught up to your plane of thought, they may have had the last thought, which was, what could you think about that as you just go walking. In the rain, where there are a few things you've never seen before, a fractal goat is getting old and a street singer is hamming it up as strong as ever before. So one is with the sweet summertime wishing you were in a ville; that you will admit it's really a reality blessing, so one may take a break from that and try a form of farm there, the light is as bright as it is fantastic, you stay with their bus. Then their bus is gassed and it really goes groovy because they take you back to where they call out the short takes and make it into a movie. You camp anywhere, anyway it's where to go, they've gotten it on and a toy train stuffs the included things into your bag. It's like that. There are these things you have got going. Tough as it may seem, it's really a once in a lifetime opportunity, then you may feel better since there is food for the day.

Projection Masquerade

To go too far in the late projection-sound that sets it so, it's okay.

Masquerading, a little girl spoke of speaking, a speak language. All so the heavenly maidens, ladies who swim through the maze of a forest like birds, doves, see balloons. Blue-green balloons are there. The little girl keeps to the bleak side for good reasons, it's a frozen outside, where a statue is masquerading as a little girl who squeaks about maidens in a forest of balloons.

Half a Circus

A person resting on the shore where airplanes fly-by, watched his day. It was the day all the kids were gay, and they are posing on a tightrope as dogs bark in annoyance to them. Some men and women are dancing as cats are dancing, stomp on the ceiling is above. All this is turning with the dogs barking, and Slim, the songwriter's swan yells, it's a moving thing. As then, heavy seashells line the center ring, the divers who got them switch to an on, right on thing, at the switch, like a railroad track switch by the center ring.

Listening There

Listening for the meditation, sitting there in a chair, a psychiatrist is listening to the record of truth; his patient is revealing his deepest, darkest thoughts. Then life flows naturally, all around them, the mistakes in the life that flows are the nominal ones which seem to be in the truth, where no mistakes can get to.

Deep

So very deep in you, in your mind, in your heart, you may see the very best of a little bit of a mind place where you may be in that which you see, and find little bits of the scene. You try and come to the mental place and try not to be too late. It's okay, in your heart, in your mind; you're where you are at, which is where it's at.

The Hand of Fate

The hand of fate calls for you, you're someone waiting to do what they do. You wait out fate, it's drawing near, and you have a healthy fear. You're free to go in any direction that goes past the scene. Next time, it's like the face of rest is the fate that allows you to do your best. You do that.

Heaven

Consuming the time, mists of heaven let you believe it is open for you. The strong and weak who refute this are into agelessness. These have correspondences to the magic, mistaking magic for heaven is the repentant element of time. In the repetition of the faith, rain on earth is having a time. Again with feasts, and spread for you. Then there, time remains a span off of the event. The mystery of the words goes to the wisdom of them. The past, a blanket, less pictorial view is positive there is a serene, peaceful air in the openness that is there.

Wonderful Wonder

The moment of amazement in the wonderful, magical misty morning lights gets one to gazing at the water of its bubbling; and waves are liquid, squeezed. You're by the side, cooking over wood burning, the fire for that is working. Later, you're reading a book in a warm chair, it's bringing you to keeping the view of the stream, now giving a mist, a view that if followed goes to the cool ocean, which is lighted with plankton. Yesterday there were turtle trails in the phosphorescent organisms we admire. They can be friendly.

A carriage comes on an old road near the stream and you wonder if its wheels are turning, it glides on by, and it's on an old road that goes by a cliff where a waterfall careens toward the sea. As the horses pull the carriage along, there, your eyes twinkle and you sigh. There they are listening to the waterfall. It's a sight to see them rest, when the great work of pulling the carriage is growing into the way the pull. The motley mob in the carriage are calling to the horses, its driver sways to the side. They go on to a distant fork in the road, wandering on and you come to wonder if the stream is feeding the waterfall.

Always

Always is allowing there to be a watcher to watch over us, there to protect us, like an eagle and like a dove, protecting a forest and a mountain, a flower and a tree, is taking countless times to just be for those who put it some other way. And I would chance to find the way among the flowers, and become long into the existence of the sea, the hollow in the tree stump, the tall sea wave by time of days shading, existing to gain the in-between of themselves, life among the tall trees, like a sailing ship's mast, always as so many days going on are gone.

Beside the Hand

Beside some tabled paraphernalia, assorted works of things that weren't written by one whose night was not there, there was the vision.

That night, there was a hand over the scene, it was shadowy. As one turned the pages of a book they read, the hand turned to mist then nothing.

Psych

An unconscious fantasy came to the news; a bard was reading fourteen poems in one day. Seven stars of the bard's part of the sky were above the door to the house of the scene. They were halfway to the far distant sky and it was a new thing to interest the inhabitants there.

As calm as the inhabitants were there, the stars switched to speedy departure as the world of the scene was unknown to them. The stars becoming the new worlds were calm, they helped the environment.

Word

One day was there to find words; they were of one mind, kind in being there of reason and prone to new ideas. That which may confuse the mind was so self-assured that the words being facilitated by the word of the mind, tarries with a word.

Threads of Thought

Threads of thought once in a while, they catch each other, once in a pile. Then, like sewing, we rely on those threads that are going, like thoughts; we have to make it through to another time later on. The threads of thought may say so, must we wear now that we are going? And so it's the entire song, and sewers weave threads of thought so we will have them to wear. In time we do find the threads of thought in a song. We thought they were for a cloth, we thought that could be. The threads were where they should be, on a spool, yet, doing what the threads that would be worn, as the threads of thought were there and yet could be getting worn; and wearing.

To Think

To think about people to talk to, tapestries, and screens, if they could only see through the words and a lot of the dreams. To tell tales and be reaching for it, like it's a bit off a date, then that's how reaching there may be, but it doesn't mean being late. It's to the terms that tell us there is so much in the tales, all told, it's so we go on to see, to get, to be, and to cool, for almost all worldly ways are, too, told.

Hint of Thought Flight

The view of two hundred days and wind are in the mind, a bird that flew through five of the days has a bell about its neck and parades with a tail wind. As through the next view, a man who jumps through the ceiling went to sing, where a hand that is just off the door knob is appearing, thought flew.

As I thought a thought three thousand times, like a bird that was a plane thought, there were a thousand times a pear tree and a service dog, and talking between these got worse as time was too bad. That's when they thought flight disappeared, flying like a thought was meanwhile a thought, it was it is flying.

He, Someplace

Someplace is masculine. He is the lighthouse by the big house by it, where he stays till the days have gone on. The trail there is where one sings. Before and after, a hand is there to come through time as awareness of it is flowing on into rhyme.

Gone to the End

False start, yelled the coach and the runners came back to the line. The start resumed and went to a happy horizon as the miles of the marathon were there. Where the thin winds wound past the merry couples, trios, and singles running, all together, forever of a day that was dawning, they went to the parching of the sun, its cloud edges like molding. Within the time they were the self, melted together as metals of a highway sign in the sun, the finish loomed.

Postcards

A picture postcard, like a big-view vision, was passed to a receiver; the big window of its picture worried the person who was the receiver of the postcard. The big, blue sky shone through an open window as the rocking chair rocked through time till it got there. A wicker basket to the side caught the windy parcel as the card was passed on to the small box.

Amid A Stock

Once, a person sitting amid a chaotic stock of papers and files in a business administration office pondered a lot. To be gazing at a spot on a pile of the stock, while waiting for a spot on the pile to be there, the person spied eyes aiming at them. Before they stopped sitting amid the stock, they asked quite a lot of the stock. For then, they could see the spot.

Halo Tale

The vision of a halo was gold, it was found to be a weight. The gold of it was found and someone became old in the cold, saw the wind going by with mist, and heard the words that were in the halo. They may be seen with their eyes. It says, you there, halo wearer, there. It's all aglow now, but so good.

See

Have you an idea about what you want to be, are you in space and time? So what have you in mind? A thought, a word, a man, a bird, a tree? More likely, a fireman, a doctor, a soldier, a musician.

Or when you want to be, at a scheduled job screening, or participating in a sporting event? Are you thinking, then, it would be sitting for a portrait?

Should you find out who you are, then that's what kind of person you want to be, like happy, good, studious, thin, and bizarre? Are you who you want to be? Have you been wondering what kind of person you might want to be? You can find out. Never mind the time, see.

Have you no perspective on the matter?

Since you have got to be free of things like sugar peas, and you want to be with the many people there are that one can see, and if one does, there's a way one can find out who they are. It's simple, see. And if that gets me wondering then, who might be in the blessing then, there's that which you want to be. You can find out, just see. It's easy to be and see. See.

So have a perspective and be free, be what you want to be and when you see. There is a way, see.

Sometimes we have perspectives about it, but then, see.

The June Bug's Humming

Humming of the June bug that hailed time came from that which had come to it, it was a humming bug. As it was humming it went along to a plumb dumped, riding way. On that, the way which was as truthful as tuneful, it was buzzing. While a girl of a forest directed the June bug for its avoidance of its going through it all, going to the well thought clue, without having made sense to you, having marvels of the now, the girl marveled at it all and waited for more than a time in which one could do all that going through.

But to go through and on to a place of mind, in which more than one can do is what they're doing, the hummer knows you can go through a river to make it to the other side. Flowing on it, you may go there while it keeps humming by the shore there, where it seems that it's all in the now. It just keeps going on, humming as it's going through a scene. It goes into a television screen, which takes its toll on the time. Time to see it through and humming will get one through. Then, humming as one sees it, one goes slightly toward where there is a way through. It's something, humming.

It's humming that's coming towards you, while waiting words are there, right by the time that is so there. Meanwhile, it's better off in the blues. Thus, humming is what gets you where you may have a humming good time to be, though buzzing is not what it seems; humming is a way to a means.

Scene

The beach was a scene, with a pulpit in the sand dune, traditional-like sand in the wind blowing so. The scene includes those who are fat, thin, and in-between. In the nearby surf, waves of various sizes are breaking there. And like in a dream, supporting the scene, dear maidens sit coyly looking toward the sea. Also, blinking their eyes is a man. He stands close up to those others of various shapes and sizes. They are there with their female partners. In the breeze the lover pair sits in a canoe, it's being paddled by the strong, young men who get it going steadily. A porpoise leaps nearby them into the sky. A flower lei is draped from its bow. Nearby, a sailing ship continues on its way.

Hardly noticed in the ship's shallow crow's nest, a farther out whale breach is exciting for the day. A nest in the crow's nest hosts a sea bird. A large sea bird hosts the pulpit, it is perched there. Then the surf is breaking further out. On the horizon are seen small white water waves. Flowers are everywhere about the scene, the beach with its waves rolling in at the sunset. And with darkness setting in, the day and its waves go to the past. A single wave crests near shore and breaks and rolls on and on past the pulpit, and on and on to the beach end.

Thoughts

Psyching the many thoughts of a tribe that contemplated whispers, what it doesn't come down to is the voice that does so goes on the wind. It's nothing but a thought in a while. A thought that is a whisper is of hundreds of thoughts. The words of it may be in images formed of the thoughts that don't whisper. Organized thinkers think, only by the voice can whispers be. One day at a time, the wind, but a thought is thinking in a thought. And since it forms words and imaginative images, it, just as organized as someone can be, goes, thinkers speak their thoughts. Those whose thought was cool are those whose thinking does what it ought to do.

Imagine

Imagining an engine, the mind is full. An empty house is imagined by a mouth and a sky's imagined by a mind. To allow oneself a lot of hope, should a mind be thinking of a joke? Then one's head of nose, ears, eyes, hair, mouth, and all feel hope, allowing yourself to be rescued of the thought that takes the hope with them. With one who is all the way in laughter, you feel what you have. To stick to your hope, you may learn of your hopes, may a breath breathe of hope. Then the dream of hope is imagined as if your hope is in the view. The toke is a view of water, it's pretty and a place to stay, it's small where the mystic meadow is and you are there to play with window shades, beaches and rocks. One imagines a rambling way, you run away with it; you travel to a nice place to stay. It's a stage. Nowhere imagines the rambler that takes you on to a hat full of imagination, it rains on you and you take to a nearby beach where the seaweed is. It stays in your idea, you capture the day, and it's laughter in the park trees. There is a group, the captain plays checkers with a hostess, and they have discussions on the end of it. The view is you see. A blue-eyed cowboy and cattle. They are where at the distance, aside a campfire, where a full moon is out of nowhere yet on the horizon, and the rescue of the view is the engine that took all to it.

Anything

Anything fast in music is what it does to you. It could be old recordings, but if they feel that fast is cool, it's cool as anything. What that feels like to you is anything that is what is, it drives you to feel life as anything. It feels like that's what it is. It feels like everything is still going well. If you follow, it's yes, but the wind. Haven't you found a speech going in the breeze? Its pompous flying is going through the trees. The wind keeping the forest so right is alright. Will it be alright with you? You go on having fun, seeking serious musicians with some pleasing, pleasant to be of a please. But it's in the breeze, yet it is that true anything new. If it's true, it's true if it's doing something, yet it was anything. Since it's anything, it's anything because some went at such a pace.

Bead Counting

If someone is counting their beads and they should be doing, some look more closely.

If someone is somewhere else than right there, and it's what there is to do; to them it's why else should someone be mentally multitasking the morning, counting beads in rounds? It's something to do. There are natural pauses in thought so early in the morning, some sound bead rounds are found going round to where they were. When they be a somewhere, that would be so close, then there is something in a pause that may bring this to a vision, also.